NEBRASKA

Julie Murray

Big Buddy BOOKS
Explore the United States

VISIT US AT
www.abdopublishing.com

Published by ABDO Publishing Company, PO Box 398166, Minneapolis, MN 55439.

Printed in the United States of America, North Mankato, Minnesota.
042012
092012

 PRINTED ON RECYCLED PAPER

Coordinating Series Editor: Rochelle Baltzer
Editor: Sarah Tieck
Contributing Editors: Megan M. Gunderson, BreAnn Rumsch, Marcia Zappa
Graphic Design: Adam Craven
Cover Photograph: *Shutterstock*: Weldon Schloneger.
Interior Photographs/Illustrations: *AP Photo*: AP Photo (p. 23), Lincoln Journal Star/FRANCIS GARDLER (pp. 21, 26), North Wind Picture Archives via AP Images (p. 13); *Getty Images*: Jodi Cobb/National Geographic (p. 17), Robert Cross/Chicago Tribune/MCT via Getty Images (p. 27), Rex Hardy Jr./Time Life Pictures (p. 25); *Glow Images*: Imagebroker RM (p. 19); *iStockphoto*: ©iStockphoto.com/Chushkin (p. 30), ©iStockphoto.com/MidwestWilderness (p. 5), ©iStockphoto.com/outtakes (p. 30); *Shutterstock*: George Burba (p. 27), Helenlbuxton (p. 27), Philip Lange (p. 30), Melanie Metz (p. 17), Caitlin Mirra (pp. 26, 29), Henryk Sadura (p. 11), Weldon Schloneger (p. 19), Steve Shoup (p. 30), Suzanne Tucker (p. 9).

All population figures taken from the 2010 US census.

Library of Congress Cataloging-in-Publication Data

Murray, Julie, 1969-
  Nebraska / Julie Murray.
     p. cm. -- (Explore the United States)
  ISBN 978-1-61783-365-6
  1. Nebraska--Juvenile literature. I. Title.
  F666.3.M872 2012
  978.2--dc23
                          2012007220

NEBRASKA

Contents

One Nation

The United States is a **diverse** country. It has farmland, cities, coasts, and mountains. Its people come from many different backgrounds. And, its history covers more than 200 years.

Today the country includes 50 states. Nebraska is one of these states. Let's learn more about this state and its story!

Did You Know?

Nebraska became a state on March 1, 1867. It was the thirty-seventh state to join the nation.

Nebraska is known for its rich farmland.

Nebraska Up Close

The United States has four main **regions**. Nebraska is in the Midwest.

Nebraska has six states on its borders. South Dakota is north. Iowa is east, and Missouri is southeast. Kansas is south. Colorado is southwest, and Wyoming is west.

Nebraska has a total area of 77,349 square miles (200,333 sq km). About 1.8 million people live there.

REGIONS OF THE UNITED STATES

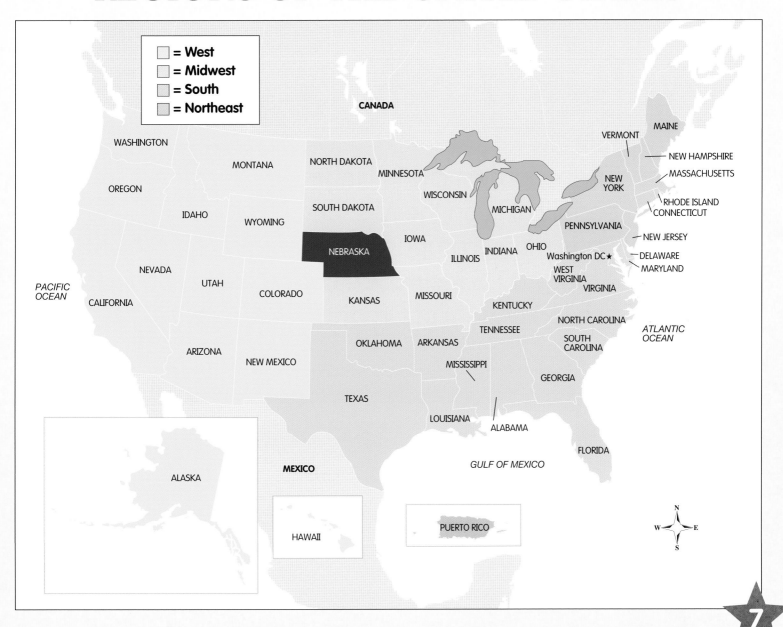

= West
= Midwest
= South
= Northeast

CANADA

WASHINGTON
MONTANA
NORTH DAKOTA
MINNESOTA
OREGON
IDAHO
WYOMING
SOUTH DAKOTA
WISCONSIN
MICHIGAN
NEW YORK
VERMONT
MAINE
NEW HAMPSHIRE
MASSACHUSETTS
RHODE ISLAND
CONNECTICUT
NEW JERSEY
PENNSYLVANIA
IOWA
NEBRASKA
NEVADA
UTAH
COLORADO
KANSAS
ILLINOIS
INDIANA
OHIO
Washington DC ★
DELAWARE
MARYLAND
WEST VIRGINIA
VIRGINIA
MISSOURI
PACIFIC OCEAN
CALIFORNIA
KENTUCKY
TENNESSEE
NORTH CAROLINA
ATLANTIC OCEAN
ARIZONA
NEW MEXICO
OKLAHOMA
ARKANSAS
SOUTH CAROLINA
MISSISSIPPI
GEORGIA
TEXAS
LOUISIANA
ALABAMA
FLORIDA
ALASKA
MEXICO
GULF OF MEXICO
HAWAII
PUERTO RICO

N
W E
S

7

IMPORTANT CITIES

Omaha is the largest city in Nebraska. It is home to 408,958 people. It is on the Missouri River.

This city has many companies that make food. Also, one of the biggest US **insurance** companies is based there. It is called Mutual of Omaha.

Nebraska

Omaha
Bellevue
Lincoln ★

Gene Leahy Mall is a popular park in downtown Omaha. It has a playground, a waterway, and an outdoor theater.

Lincoln is Nebraska's **capital**. It is also the second-largest city in the state, with 258,379 people. The University of Nebraska–Lincoln is located there.

Bellevue is the state's third-largest city, with 50,137 people. It is home to the Offutt Air Force Base and many parks.

The Nebraska State Capitol is one of four state capitols shaped like a skyscraper.

NEBRASKA IN HISTORY

Nebraska's history includes Native Americans, **pioneers**, and settlers. Native Americans have lived in present-day Nebraska for thousands of years. In the 1800s, pioneers began traveling through this area on the Oregon Trail.

In 1862, a new law gave people free land in the Midwest and West. Many settlers came to the Nebraska Territory to claim land. In 1867, Nebraska became a state.

Did You Know?

Today, a monument in Beatrice honors settlers who claimed nearby land.

Families traveled the Oregon Trail to claim land in the West. They passed through what is now Nebraska.

Timeline

1803

President Thomas Jefferson bought land from France that included what is now Nebraska. This was called the **Louisiana Purchase**.

1854

Nebraska became a US territory.

1800s

American explorers Meriwether Lewis and William Clark visited Nebraska.

1804

Fort Atkinson was established. Nebraska's first school and first library were built there.

1819

Nebraska became the thirty-seventh state on March 1.

1867

14

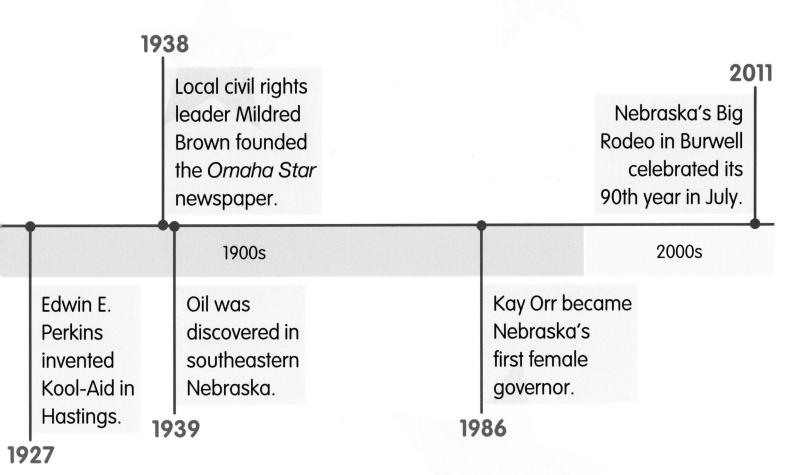

1938

Local civil rights leader Mildred Brown founded the *Omaha Star* newspaper.

2011

Nebraska's Big Rodeo in Burwell celebrated its 90th year in July.

1900s

2000s

Edwin E. Perkins invented Kool-Aid in Hastings.

Oil was discovered in southeastern Nebraska.

Kay Orr became Nebraska's first female governor.

1939

1986

1927

ACROSS THE LAND

Nebraska has farmland, **plains**, streams, and rivers. Major rivers include the Missouri and the Platte. The Great Plains cover the middle and western parts of the state. Nebraska also has the country's largest area of sand **dunes**.

Many types of animals make their homes in Nebraska. These include coyotes, mule deer, and pheasants.

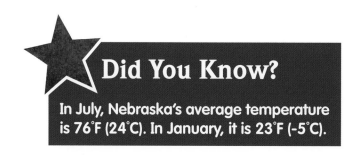

Did You Know?

In July, Nebraska's average temperature is 76°F (24°C). In January, it is 23°F (-5°C).

Nebraska can have wild weather. Tornadoes may touch down in the summer (*left*). And blizzards can happen in the winter.

The Sand Hills area in central Nebraska has grass-covered sand dunes.

17

Earning a Living

Nebraska has many important businesses. These include farms and companies that make food. Many people work for **insurance** companies. And, some people have jobs helping visitors to the state.

Many businesses move goods through Nebraska. The state has well-connected freeways and roads. It also has railroads, an important airport, and river ports.

18

Corn (*left*), beef cattle, and hogs are important Nebraska farm products.

Bailey Yard in North Platte is the world's largest railroad yard.

19

SPORTS PAGE

Many people think of college sports when they think of Nebraska. The Creighton University Bluejays are known for basketball. The University of Nebraska Cornhuskers are known for football.

Did You Know?

Tom Osborne was the University of Nebraska's football coach from 1973 to 1997. He served in the US Congress from 2001 until 2007.

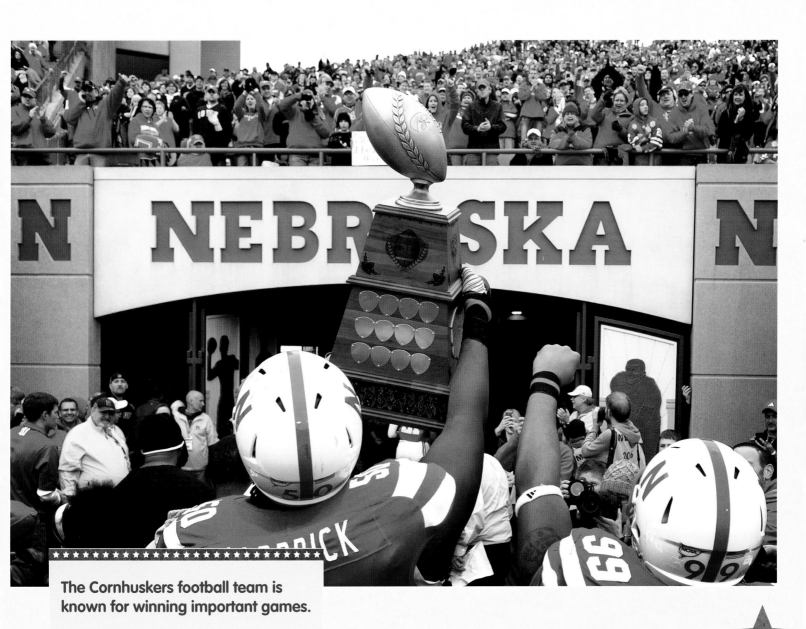

The Cornhuskers football team is known for winning important games.

HOMETOWN HEROES

Many famous people are from Nebraska. Gerald Ford was born in Omaha in 1913. He was the US president from 1974 to 1977.

Ford is the only person to be president and vice president without being elected to either office. President Richard Nixon named him vice president in 1973, when his first vice president left office. Then when Nixon left office in 1974, Ford became president.

Ford was the thirty-eighth US president.

Did You Know?

Before becoming a movie star, Astaire danced with his sister in stage shows.

Fred Astaire was born in Omaha in 1899. His real name was Fred Austerlitz. He became a famous dancer, actor, and singer in the 1920s. He worked for about 75 years! Many people still consider him one of the best dancers ever.

Ginger Rogers was Astaire's most popular dance partner.

Tour Book

Do you want to go to Nebraska? If you visit the state, here are some places to go and things to do!

Discover

See Chimney Rock. This famous rock formation is on the historic Oregon Trail.

★ Cheer

Watch the University of Nebraska Cornhuskers play football. Be sure to wear the school colors, red and white!

★ Remember

Tour William "Buffalo Bill" Cody's home in North Platte. In the late 1880s, he became famous for his Wild West show. It featured plays, cowboys, and wild animals.

★ Taste

Eat some fresh sweet corn! Nebraska is known as the Cornhusker State. That's because much of the state's land is used for growing corn.

★ See

Spend time in Omaha's Old Market. This popular historic area has brick streets.

A Great State

The story of Nebraska is important to the United States. The people and places that make up this state offer something special to the country. Together with all the states, Nebraska helps make the United States great.

Scotts Bluff is in western Nebraska. It helped mark the path for travelers on the Oregon Trail.

29

Fast Facts

Date of Statehood:
March 1, 1867

Population (rank):
1,826,341
(38th most-populated state)

Total Area (rank):
77,349 square miles
(16th largest state)

Motto:
"Equality Before the Law"

Nickname:
Cornhusker State,
Beef State

State Capital:
Lincoln

Flag:

Flower: Giant Goldenrod

Postal Abbreviation:
NE

Tree: Eastern Cottonwood

Bird: Western Meadowlark

Important Words

capital a city where government leaders meet.

diverse made up of things that are different from each other.

dune a hill or ridge of loose sand piled up by the wind.

fort a building with strong walls to guard against enemies.

insurance a contract that promises to guard people against a loss of money if something happens to them or their property.

Louisiana Purchase land the United States purchased from France in 1803. It extended from the Mississippi River to the Rocky Mountains and from Canada through the Gulf of Mexico.

pioneer one of the first people to settle on new land.

plains flat or rolling land without trees.

region a large part of a country that is different from other parts.

Web Sites

To learn more about Nebraska, visit ABDO Publishing Company online. Web sites about Nebraska are featured on our Book Links page. These links are routinely monitored and updated to provide the most current information available.

www.abdopublishing.com

Index